# DEDICATION

This book is dedicated to my wife Seneca Shackleford, the queen of my life, who has been there for me whenever I've needed you. Your encouragement, empathy, faith, love and warm sense of humor, has nourished and supported me through the most difficult period of my life. You have enriched my understanding of love immeasurably . . . and for this, I am grateful.

# Eating My Way To
# Heaven

*Living an Unhealthy Life Could Kill You*

# Eating My Way To **Heaven**

*Living an Unhealthy Life Could Kill You*

## Robert J. Shackleford

ASA Publishing Corporation

ASA Publishing Corporation
1285 N. Telegraph Rd., #376, Monroe, Michigan 48162
*An Accredited Publishing House with the BBB*
www.asapublishingcorporation.com

All Rights Reserved. No part of this publication may be reproduced, stored in a retrieval system or transmitted in any form or by any means electronic, mechanical, photocopying, recording or otherwise, without the prior written permission of the publisher. Author/writer rights to "Freedom of Speech" protected by and with the "1st Amendment" of the Constitution of the United States of America. This is a work of non-fiction Christian educational health. Any resemblance to actual events, locales, person living or deceased that is not related to the author's literacy is entirely coincidental.

With this title/copyright page, the reader is notified that the publisher does not assume, and expressly disclaims any obligation to obtain and/or include any other information other than that provided by the author except with permission. Any belief system, promotional motivations, including but not limited to the use of non-fictional/fictional characters and/or characteristics of this book, are within the boundaries of the author's own creativity in order to reflect the nature and concept of the book. Unless otherwise indicated, all scripture quotations are taken from the King James Version of the Bible.

Any and all vending sales and distribution not permitted without full book cover and this copyright page.

Copyrights©2019 Robert J. Shackleford, All Rights Reserved
Book Title: Eating My Way To Heaven *Living an Unhealthy Life Could Kill You*
Date Published: 01.05.2019 / Edition 1 *Trade Paperback*
Book ID: ASAPCID2380771
ISBN: 978-1-946746-47-4
Library of Congress Cataloging-in-Publication Data

This book was published in the United States of America.
Great State of Michigan

## Table of Contents

**Acknowledgements** ...................................................(a)

**Introduction** ..................................................................1

**Chapter 1**
    Prepare The Whole Man .......................................5

**Chapter 2**
    Man's Way of Being Healthy ...............................13

**Chapter 3**
    God's Way for Man To Be Healthy .....................21
        Eat Right ........................................................23
        Exercise .........................................................30
        Rest.................................................................35

**Chapter 4**
    Where Did It Come From ....................................37
        High Blood Pressure ......................................41
        Arthritis .........................................................43
        Heart Disease ................................................44

**Chapter 5**
    How to Stay Healthy............................................47
        Reeducate .....................................................48
        Losing Weight................................................49
        How to Keep The Weight Off ........................55

- The Food We Eat ..................................................... 55
- Vitamin A ............................................................... 56
- Vitamin B1 (Thiamine) ............................................ 56
- Vitamin B2 (Riboflavin) ........................................... 57
- Vitamin B6 (Pyridoxine) .......................................... 58
- Vitamin B12 (Cyanocobalamin) ............................... 58
- Vitamin C (Ascorbic Acid) ........................................ 59
- Vitamin D ............................................................... 60
- Vitamin E ............................................................... 60
- Vitamin K ............................................................... 61
- Niacin (Nicotinic Acid) ............................................ 61
- Protein (Amino Acids) ............................................ 62
- Minerals ................................................................ 63
- Calcium .................................................................. 63
- Chlorine ................................................................. 64
- Magnesium ............................................................ 64
- Phosphorus ............................................................ 65
- Potassium .............................................................. 65
- Sodium .................................................................. 66
- Sulfur ..................................................................... 66
- Copper ................................................................... 67
- Iodine .................................................................... 67
- Iron ........................................................................ 67
- Manganese ............................................................ 68
- Zinc ........................................................................ 68

**Chapter 6**
- Let's Talk .................................................................. 69
  - Bad Habits ............................................................ 73
  - Bad Traditions ...................................................... 74
  - Back To The Basics ............................................... 75

**Chapter 7**
- Good Recipes ............................................................ 77
  - Stir-Fry Vegetables with Brown Rice ................... 79
  - Cabbage 'n Corn Soup ......................................... 80
  - Red Lentil-Squash Soup ....................................... 81
  - Baked Fish with Mushroom Sauce ...................... 82
  - Mushroom Sauce ................................................. 83

**Chapter 8**
- Testimonies .............................................................. 85

**Chapter 9**
- Change Your Mind .................................................... 87
  - How To Change Your Mind ................................. 92
  - Feed Your Mind .................................................... 92
  - Strengthen Your Body .......................................... 95
  - Find A Role Model ................................................ 97
  - Repetition Is Powerful ......................................... 100
  - Mushroom Sauce ................................................. 83

**Selected Bibliography** .................................................. 103

**About the Author** ....................................................................... 105

# ACKNOWLEDGEMENTS

I would like to take this opportunity to express my gratitude to the following people:

My wonderful six children for loving me, always believing in me and for the sacrifice they made by allowing me to complete this project.

My mother and father, who loved and prayed for me throughout the years. And especially for putting up with my foolishness, while growing up as a child.

My church family, Greater Whole Truth Church, for praying and supporting me throughout the years. I love you saints.

John Little, my trainer and friend for helping me make my dreams come true. And more importantly for knowing that this book needed to be written.

And special thanks to my Doctor Richard Grutz, you are the best. your advice has help me to stay focus on growing older healthy.

# INTRODUCTION

By His stripes we are healed . . . (Isa 53:5). I am sure you have heard this by now. I have also heard this scripture quoted a million times in the Pentecostal church I grew up in as a child. I have seen long prayer lines for healing from sickness that people brought on themselves. I have seen some of the same people back in the healing line again, after they said they were healed. I know if Jesus carried all of my sickness, then why I'm sick? This is a good question. I hope you find the answer in this book. But be warned: What you will read in this book may shock your beliefs about healing. This is precisely why I had to write this book, for my beliefs were also shocked about healing.

Please understand that I too, suffered from acne and sinus problems; headaches, and being overweight. As a matter of fact, evangelist, and pastors-almost everyone it seems, prayed for me to get healed. They even told me that I was healed. But instead I got worse. Why? It wasn't that I didn't have faith, but I was simply violating what Jesus Had already done on Calvary.

Now many of you who are so spiritual would say that, "the devil made me sick." What I am about to say may make you close this book and put it in the garbage. But I don't think so. Just give me a chance to explain myself. God didn't make me sick nor did the devil. Well, who did it? I did it.

Like most African-Americans, my diet was not the kind of diet that would keep me healthy inside and out. I ate what they called "soul food" and "junk food." It's death food. In the chapters ahead, I'll explain what I'm talking about.

I was also addicted to sugar. But I was preaching against those who were addicted to smoking and drinking etc. I know that two wrongs do not make a right. I was feeling like I was dying, but still preaching that Jesus took my infirmities (sickness) and carried my sorrows (Isa. 53:4). But then the day came, when I discovered who my real enemy was, and I begin to fight back. I was my enemy. My way, traditions and habits were also my enemies. I then begin to walk out my healing and live a fruitful life. No healing lines, no prayer cloths, no laying-your-hand-on-my-hand kind of thing. I didn't need that anymore. I just believed God's Word and lived it.

To those of you who are sick, I have learned that if you just believe God's word and live it, you too will walk in perfect health. So, find a nice chair, relax, and have an open mind . . . Because your gateway to divine healing is right before you.

# CHAPTER 1

## *Preparing The Whole Man*

Many of us Christians are well versed in the Bible. We pray every day and really love God. But we are not taking diligent care of the body God has given us. The Bible says, "Now may the God of peace Himself sanctify you entirely; and may your spirit and body be preserved complete, without blame at the coming of our Lord Jesus Christ." (I Thess. 5:23) Most of us are focus on the spirit man and that's fine, however there must be a balance.

The human man consists of spirit, soul and body. All three dimensions must be taking care of. But the devil doesn't want God's people to be prepared, well and sound. You see Satan will attack us from a different angle or wait for a time when we do not have our armor in its proper place.

Ephesians 6:11 says, "put on the whole armor of God, that you may be able to stand against the wiles of the devil." The word wiles don't mean that the devil is a wild man in the sense of being able to jump twenty buses on a motorcycle. But the Greek word for wiles is "method" it denotes craft, deceit, a cunning device. The Greek word for "wiles" could have been translated "methods." Satan has many demonically-devised methods and schemes to outwit the child of God. Therefore, we must have the mind of Christ and the power of the Spirit, if we are going to overcome Satan's methods.

One of his method is to stop you from hearing and knowing the truth. Satan doesn't want us to know the truth about our bodies. The Bible says, "stand therefore having your loins girt about with truth (Eph. 6:14). To have our "loins" girt about with truth is to have the living and written word controlling our lives. The believer who loves the truth and live it, will have a strong spiritual life. This is truth, God wants your spirit, soul and body whole. He wants us to walk in complete health: physical, mental, emotional, and spiritual wholeness, is

God's will for our lives. The whole man must be made whole, in order to be a better witness.

There is a great verse in the Bible that says, "Beloved, I wish above all things that thou mayest proper and be in health, even as thy soul prosper" (3 John 2). John was writing to Gaius. He earnestly prayed that this beloved brother would prosper and be as well off physically as he was spiritually. John was concerned about the health of this believing brother. He wanted him to enjoy the blessing of a strong body and to stay physically fit, to be a good soldier in the army of Christ Jesus.

The Apostle John said . . . that thou mayest prosper . . . the Greek word here translated "prosper" holds the meaning that John desired success and happiness in the man of God's life. Success in business, in domestic relations, and any other transaction in which a Christian might become engaged.

The source of such success is God. Seeking after God and not success will cause us to prosper. The Bible says, "as long as the king sought the Lord, God gave him success" (2 Chron. 26:5). Uzziah was sixteen years old when he became king and he reigned in Jerusalem fifty-two years. And if he sought the Lord, God made him prosper. But one day pride got in his way and he started to seek things and not God. The bottom line is that he fell real hard. We must seek God in order that we may have a successful life.

Many people want to have a stronger mind, so they get into meditation, drugs, and various kinds of reading materials. Most people want to have a better physical body, so they resort to doing all types of crazy things. But I will talk more about the body in the next chapter. The truth is that if we do it God's way, there will be less sick people.

It is very important that you take care of the whole man (spirit, soul, body). Now if you really want to be spiritual, then find out how you can be a healthy person. I used to hear this phrase as a little boy coming up in the church, "singing and shouting is fine, but it is the word of God that will keep you." That is so true. But many of us are too spiritual to see that God want us to be healthy. You must take care of yourself (spirit, soul, body).

Preparation takes time and discipline when you want to keep the whole person healthy. Nobody can do it for you and nobody can want it for you. It is your spirit, soul and body so own up to it and begin to prepare for a better you. Preparation must start in your mind if you want a better and healthy you. So many of us sit on the couch and watch workout programs on television wishing that slim healthy person was you. Wishing and preparing are two different things. Wishing does not make you healthy and whole, but preparing your spirit, soul, and body for a better you will. Anybody can say "I want to eat healthy and exercise today,' but an unprepared mind will not make you healthy.

How many of us will drive a car that has a good motor, but the transmission is bad? The transmission will not allow you to reverse, how frustrating that is. Many of us are like this car, we say that our bodies are prepared for a healthy life. You say that your heart is healthy, but your lungs are full of cigarette smoke. You say that your weight is perfect, but you continue to eat sugary foods, knowing that you are diabetic. You say that your mind is healthy, but your thought pattern is so negative. You say prayer is the key to staying healthy, but you will not spend time in prayer. Again, preparation takes time and is the key to a better you.

I get so excited when I hear about a person who are well discipline in eating healthier, working hard in keeping a healthy mind, and having a healthy body. I know that it takes a strong person to work at it every day. I know that it takes a discipline person to work at it every day. Many of you deserve a discipline award for your heroic effort in fighting off negativity from entering your mind. Getting up every day to work out when your body wants to stay in the bed, I say you deserve the discipline award. You and I know that eating a bowl of ice cream and a bag a chip late at night sounds so good to the flesh. However, you are well discipline to fight off those urges. Again, you deserve the discipline award. You are a significant role model for others in being discipline in taking care of the whole person. I take my hat off to you, because I personally know that it is not easy to be discipline in a world we live in today. Keep up the magnificent work of being discipline.

If I take a survey asking 100 people in a room who want to go to heaven, how many hands would raise up? Let me answer it for you. Everybody in the room will have their hands up. Can I get a witness? Well I want to tell you how you can get to heaven quick and fast. Stay depressed and keep running to comfort food like ice cream, cake, salty potato chips, donuts, and the famous thick cheese burger. Depression will tell you to close the curtains and eat these kinds of foods late at night, and by eating like this you will get sick and die. Knowing you have hypertension and are overweight, you decided to eat salty foods and add more salt to it. You decided to not exercise and sit up at night to eat these salty foods. I know you can't wait to see Jesus. Well you are on the right track to heaven. Sooner or later you will get sick and die. You are the same person who believe that God want us healed and in good health. You are the same person who teach and preach that God did not make us poor and sick. Well why are you in a hurry to get where Jesus is (heaven)? Let us enjoy heaven on earth right now by being a good Stewart of what God has given us. He has given us health in our spirit, soul, and body.

# CHAPTER 2

## *Man's Way of Being Healthy*

Many years ago, my daughter was born weighing 3lbs. and 8oz. she was so small just like a little baby doll. However, there was one incident that I will never forget about my daughter. When she was about 9 months, a lady from the church that I was attending told me to bring her over to the house, so she could make my baby healthy. The lady from my church said she was going to feed my baby some collard greens with salt pork in it, chitterlings, ham hocks, bacon etc. I told her no way because my baby is already in good health plus she is just 9 months old. Just because she is a little small 9-month baby doesn't mean she is sick and unhealthy. Must I tell you the lady from my church was always sick and going back and forth to the hospital.

But why? Because black American tradition teaches us that good old soul food cooking will make you good and healthy. You may ask, what tradition? Well, let me just wet your appetite. Traditionally breakfast consisted of biscuits, pancakes, sausage, bacon, fried eggs, gravy, ham and chicken. I can truly go on and name much more in what is consumed during breakfast time, but I will stop. We do not eat much fruit, and not enough food that is high in fiber and we do not eat low fat food for breakfast that is high in good nutrients. Now what is consumed at dinner looks like this: fried pork chops, fried chicken, hamburgers, ham hocks, chitterlings, fried fish, over cooked veggies, ox tails, and much more. Now this is our traditional way of eating (black Americans).

Now most of us are not cooking the food in a healthy way or we shouldn't be eating it. Well you may be saying I know how to cook in a healthy way. All I am saying is you may not be cooking your food in a way that keeps most of your nutrients and that is healthy for you. For example, in macaroni and cheese; the macaroni is processed and that's not good for you. The cheese is processed too and it's high in fat, sodium, and cholesterol. Also, most of us put more salt, whole milk and eggs in it. Now with these ingredients, do you think this is healthy eating? I think not. So just because we as a people are eating good, it doesn't mean we are healthy.

Many of us are really eating our way to heaven. Meaning we are eating in a way which will send us to the emergency room or even to our own funeral. We sing about heaven and can't wait to go there, and we sing about seeing Jesus' face. You sing about the streets paved with gold and the pearly 12 gates. I got some good news for you, the doctor told you to stop, your body told you to stop, and your love ones told you to stop. But you want to go see Jesus in heaven so bad that you can't stop treating yourself the way you do. So, the good news is you may be getting what you ask for. "I want to go to heaven soon by abusing my whole person" (spirit soul and body).

Did you know that 75 percent of African Americans are unhealthy? They suffer from heart disease, high blood pressure, sugar diabetes, high cholesterol, strokes obese, etc. An article published in the Men's Health Magazine states that, African Americans not only have a higher incidence of strokes than whites or Hispanics, but African Americans who survive strokes also suffer significantly more severe physical impairments than whites; according to results of studies conducted at Columbia and Duke Universities.

Overall, the estimate of the occurrence of strokes was nearly twice as high in African Americans compared to whites and Hispanics, comments Ralph L. Saceo, M.D. the principle author of the Columbia study. The problem he says may be that high blood pressure is more common in African Americans than in other ethnic groups. I personally think that this statement really a shame. So many of us are leaving this earth and going to heaven too soon, and leaving our loved ones hurt and lonely.

As people of color we are so gifted. We can sing, super actors, inventors, leading the sport industry, national leaders, business owners, professors, preachers and much more. We are a people who are very spiritual and religious, we know how to go through the motions. However, we are dying, because we're eating ourselves to heaven. So many of us are sick, under/overweight and eating everything that is on the table. You know, and I know that this is not a healthy thing to do, we as a people must wake up, because we have been sleeping much too long.

Later in this book I am going to talk directly to my African American family. If mom and dad are eating unhealthy and sick with diseases that they brought on themselves, then their innocent children will eat unhealthy and suffer with heart, blood and gum disease, rotten teeth, diabetes and strokes, according to statistics on African Americans. Not only our children will suffer for illness, but our children's children will suffer too, because we are eating according to the traditions of men.

Have you noticed that around Thanksgiving and Christmas that the industry starts to advertise on radio and television ways to unstop your bowels and to release the gas in you? Why? Because we overdo it during the holidays by eating everything but the kitchen sink. The doctors get very excited during the holidays because they know you are going to break all the rules and get sick from eating food that you should not be eating. Not only do the doctors get paid, but so do the drug and grocery stores. Everybody is happy except you, because you are the one who is sick.

When you eat man's way you will get sick and possibly go to heaven. We need not only read in the Bible about salvation, love, Jesus, Holy Spirit and faith. In addition, we need to read about how to take care of the whole person (spirit, soul, and body). Man's way has been proven to satisfy the desires of the flesh and will have us in bondage to what is offered to the flesh. The Bible said, there is a way which seem right unto a man, but the end thereof are the ways of death . . . Proverbs 14:12

King Nebuchadnezzar wanted healthy and intelligent men in his palace. But he wanted to make them healthy man's way by feeding them food that was contrary to what Daniel was accustomed to. So, one day the king ordered Ashpenaz, chief of his court officials to bring in some of the Israelites from the royal family. Young men without any physical defect, handsome, and skillful in all wisdom, well informed, quick to understand, and qualified to serve in the king's palace. Daniel, Meshach, Shadrach, and Abednego were included in that number.

These four boys were very healthy because they ate the food that God wanted them to eat. Even at an early age they were in good health. Why? Because their parents ate healthy and continue with the godly tradition of eating clean food. Now Daniel made up his mind that he would not defile his body with the king's choice food, and with the wine that he drank. So, he made a deal with the commander of the officials. Daniel said, please test us for ten days by giving us nothing but vegetables to eat and water to drink. So, the guard took away their choice food and the wine they were to drink and gave them vegetables instead (Daniel 1:1-15). And at the end of the ten days they looked healthier and more nourished than any of the young men who ate the royal food. I am not saying that we should eat only vegetables and drink water, but we really need to eat better than what we eat now.

Almost on every corner in America there is a fast food restaurant. It is a shame that society dictates what we should eat. Man's way of eating healthy is to eat French fries with ketchup, chili dogs with cheese, onion rings, pizza, hamburger with cheese, pop and all types of deserts. We must not let the fast food joints kill us, even though the food is so tasty. They (fast food restaurants) are getting richer, and we are getting sicker and sooner or later we will die and go to heaven. The restaurant industry does not care that you are getting out of shape, raising your cholesterol level, and getting sick. We got to take control of ourselves to live a healthy, holy and happy life. Let us not die before our time, because you have work to do and a purpose to fulfilled. The Bible has asked us a question in Ecclesiastes 7:17 that require an answer: Be not over much wicked, neither be thou foolish: why shouldest thou die before thy time?

I am convinced that man's way of being healthy does not work. So many people are in their grave because of the instruction that man has given them. It has got to be God's way or no way at all. God is the manufacture of man; therefore, He knows what is best for us. Eating ourselves to heaven is not Bible at all nor does it make any sense. So, let us use God's plan to get and stay healthy.

# CHAPTER 3

## *God's Way for Man To Be Healthy*

God has a way for man to eat and stay healthy. He made man and knows all about us and knows how the body supposed to function. So, when it does not function the way it supposed to, it means we are doing something wrong. And to make matters worse, when our bodies brake down we take it to the wrong manufacturer.

Perhaps after I tell this story about a friend of mine you will understand what I am talking about. My friend had a Toyota automobile that broke down for some reason. So he took it to the neighborhood mechanic who works on Ford cars.

When the mechanic was finished with his car it was in a worse condition than before. You see the man took his car to the wrong manufacturer. He should have taken it to the Toyota mechanic.

God know every part of the human body and know what it would take to keep us healthy. From the beginning of man's creation God had the blue print of man's body and how we should maintain it. He put what is needed in the human body so that we can live in this dimension. God know everything about the human body and He know what it takes to keep the body healthy. For example, in humans the intestine is divided into two major sections: the small intestine, which is about 6m (20 ft) long, and the large intestine, which has a larger diameter and is about 1.5m (5ft) long. He knows that it takes about six to eight hours for food to pass through your stomach and small intestine. Food then enters your large intestine (colon) for further digestion, absorption of water and finally, elimination of undigested food.

You see, our intestines are too long for us to fill it up with junk, and too long to fill it up with a lot of meat. This is why your bowel movement smell so bad. Have you noticed the smell of a newborn baby's bowel movement, opposed to an adult's? I am sorry that I had to use this kind of analogy, but I am sure you get the point.

A newborn baby drinks breast milk, or some type of formula milk. In a few months they are eating baby cereal and later vegetables from a jar. However, the adult is eating hamburger sandwich, steak, ham, pork chops, ox tails, pig feet, ribs, pizza, chitterlings, etc. Therefore, your bowels can't help but to smell like a sewer. A friend of mind had an upset stomach and had to use the bathroom to relieve his self. His bowel movement stank so bad that he fainted before the toilet was flushed. What do you think is going on in your body when you fill it up with so much junk? This is not God's way of eating and taking care of the best machine on this planet earth. God want us to eat right, exercise and get proper rest.

 EAT RIGHT

People think that they can eat any kind of way and put all kinds of junk in their body and get away with it. You may say "I am 55 years old and I love sweets. I have been eating sweets all of my life, and I am not sick yet." But I say if you keep on living and eating like that, you will have rotten teeth or no teeth at all. Also, you will get sick and die making your way to heaven.

It is a fact that consuming too much sugar is not good for you. Sugar causes a quick increase in energy, followed by a lowering of energy below the previous level. At this point mild depression is experienced by many persons indicating a lowering of the brain chemicals called "endorphins," which promotes a sense of well-being and pleasure. For these reasons, sugar interferes with the sex life and reduces its pleasure . . . oh oh! Plus, it destroys your teeth, and affects your blood and glands. Again, sooner or later if you keep on abusing your body you are going to get sick and may be eat your way to heaven.

Now there is a way which you should eat, and I know you are interested in knowing what it is. First, we need to know what God said, and what is on His menu. From the beginning God gave Adam and Eve the original, or first menu. Then God said, I give you every seed-bearing plant on the face of the whole earth and every tree that has fruit with seed in it. They will be yours for food (Gen. 1:29). You see God's original menu for our first parents were to eat vegetables, fruit, herbs, seeds, and nuts. He knows the human body and what is good for it.

He also knows what kind of food the body was originally designed to eat. For example, there are certain foods that fight against diseases: cabbage, it can lower the risk of colorectal cancer. The same with squash, sweet potatoes, and spinach. Broccoli is a cruciferous vegetable that contains indoles and isothiocyanates (substances that help reduce and prevent certain cancerous tumors) rich in carotenoids.

    Now if you eat foods that are not good for you, then your body will react accordingly. I know this is true, because I use to eat everything nonstop plus the kitchen sink. My body looked like a 9-month pregnant woman from eating so much ice cream, potato chips, a lot of fried meat, and my favorite was bacon. My doctor told me that I was gaining weight too fast. I did not have the energy to match my daily activities, nor did I have the desire to exercise. The pain I had in my knees and ankles was so terrible that I did not want to get up to do anything. I was eating my way to heaven big time, but I felt like I had more to do in life. I was still young and had a full life before me with children and a wife to enjoy. However, my body and mind were reacting to what I was feeding it.

    I believe if we use God's original menu people would be in better health. Better health will save you time and money.

Better health will make you smile more. Better health will booth your self-esteem. Better health will shorten the prayer line at church and allow you to stay in your seat and pray for others who need prayer. Gods plans for us are truly the best for His children. He said in Jeremiah 29:11 For I know the plans I have for you, declares the LORD, plans to prosper you and not harm you, plans to give you hope and a future (NIV).

Now you might be saying what about meat? Why didn't God include meat in His original menu? Well let me put it like this. When the car manufacturers make automobiles, they know what it will take for the car to run right. The original menu for automobiles to run right is gasoline in the tank. It was not designed to run on water, or milk mixed with gasoline. It may run for a minute but after that it will shut off. It is the same way with human beings, we were designed to eat according to the instructions God gave Adam.

Once again you may be saying, what about the laws God gave to the Israelites? Yes, meat was included in their menu. I must say if we use the menu God gave them, we would be much healthier than we are now. Now let us take a closer look at Israel's instructions and menu. It is important for me to start off by saying what God said in His word. You must distinguish between the holy and the common, between the unclean and the clean (NIV Lev. 10:10). I am the Lord who brought you up out of Egypt to be your God; therefore, be holy, because I am holy (NIV Lev.11:45). Do not eat anything you find already dead. You may give it to an alien living in any of your towns, and he may eat it, or you may sell it to a foreigner. But you are a people holy to the Lord your God (NIV Deut. 14:21).

As you already know, God is a holy God. He is different from all other gods. He is pure, clean, genuine, righteous and jealous. So, when He chose Israel for His people, He wanted them to be holy also. He didn't want them to be like other nations. They had to be holy or die. The way they worshipped had to be holy, even what they ate had to be a clean or a type of a holy animal. They couldn't eat what the Canaanites ate because they were so worldly in everything they did in the eyes of God.

So since they were going to a new land where other nations were, God had to teach them what and how to eat. Not only that, He knew what types of food would be good for them. For example, God said, you may eat any animal that has a split hoof completely divided and that chews the cud (NIV Lev. 11:3). You might be saying, what's so important about the split hoof and cud chewing animal? Well the animal with the split hoof release the poison that is in his body. And if it doesn't have the split hoof completely divided, all the poison is left in the animal's feet. Animals that chew the cud, have a complex 3 or 4 chambered stomach. It causes the food to digest better, and there is no poison build up in its system and the meat is cleaner.

Now God called out the names of the animals, that are poisonous or unclean: camel, coney (rock badger-a type of rabbit), rabbit, pig, etc. I encourage you to read Leviticus chapter 11. In Leviticus 11 there is a more detailed list of what God said not to eat. Even though God put clean meat in their menu, He always referred to the original menu.

For the Lord thy God bringeth thee into a good land, a land of brooks of water, of fountains and depths that spring out of valleys and pomegranates; a land of oil olive, and honey (Deut. 8:7-8). God know what is best for the body. He knows that fruit, vegetables, grain, seeds, nuts, herds, juices and water is best for mankind. Just like mom and dad knows best for their little children. It is the same with our father God.

What do you think the children of Israel ate after they came into the promise land? A hamburger sandwich, ham sandwich, pork chops, bacon, French fries, pop, candy, donuts, fried chicken? No to all of these. The bible said, and the manna ceased on the morrow after they had eaten of the old corn of the land; neither had the children of Israel manna anymore; but they did eat of the fruit of the land of Canaan that year (Joshua 5:12). One translation says . . . they ate of the produce of Canaan.

Do not be fooled by the commercials on television, advertisement on bill boards, radio and the neighborhood restaurants. Read the advertisement in the bible and you will be for sure to live a healthy life. I know for sure that God's way is the best way for us.

Well what about the New Testament? I do not mean to shock you, but it is in the New Testament also. Beloved, I wish above all things that thou mayest prosper and be in health, even as thy soul prospereth (3 John 2). The Greek word for health is hugianio. It denotes 'to be healthy, sound, in good health." This is where we get the word hygiene from. Yes, God really want His children to be in good health/hygiene. He wants your right and left ventricles, pulmonary veins, heart valves, aorta, coronary arteries and circulatory system . . . your whole heart healthy. He wants your endocrine glands healthy:

pituitary gland (master gland), thyroid gland, thymus gland, pancreas gland adrenal gland, testes (men), ovaries (women). I am truly convinced that it is God's will for me to be healthy

So, the next time you eat, please think about what God said. Since God cares about your body, you should care too. Stay on point with your health and get your yearly checkup. Do not wait until the doctor tell you how to eat because of sickness and being under and overweight. Start right now while you have a portion of health and strength and stop eating your way to heaven today.

 EXERCISE

Exercise is a word you do not hear about in the Christian world. For some reason it doesn't matter. We talk about Jesus, salvation, love, education, unity and healing. But exercise is not mentioned. What if I told you that it has some value in eating certain foods that would prevent cancer. What if I told you that it has some value in meditating on positive things. Would you do it? Of course, you would do it, because it has value. Everybody would like to do things that can make them better. Right? Well the bible said: For physical training is of some value, but godliness has value for all things, holding promise for both the present life and the life to come (NIV 1 Timothy 4:8). In this scripture there is a great spiritual and natural balance. There is value in exercising and taking care of your body. And there is value in spiritual exercising and living a godly life.

There are three main reasons why we as Christians do not exercise. First, we are too spiritual that we can't live a basic natural life. What I mean, we pray, fast, read the bible, go to church activities, and all these things are good. However, we forget about the basic things that God want us to do. Like be a good steward of what He has giving us. Second, ignorance plays a big part in this. Most of us do not know that we should exercise. For example, a man told me that Christians should not exercise. So, I asked him Why? He said the bible said so. I asked him to show me where it is in the bible. He did not show me, but he tried to quote a portion of that scripture. He said for bodily exercise profiteth little. So, I told him that I will go home and study the entire chapter where that passage he tried to quote. And I did.

I found out that he was totally ignorant of what it really meant. So, I went back to explain to him what I discovered.

Because physical training is of some value-useful for a little; but godliness (spiritual training) is useful and of value in everything and in every way, for it holds promise for the present life and for the life which is to come (Amp. 1 Timothy 4:8). Apostle Paul was instructing Timothy about Apostasy, and in that he was dealing with spiritual godly training. Because in verse 7 he said train yourself toward godliness (deity) - keeping yourself spiritually fit. So, he was not putting exercise down. But he was making a good point about spiritual training.

And finally, it was not in our up-bringing. How many times did you see mom and dad exercise together? Let me answer that for myself. Not one time in my life. Many of our parents left it up to the gym teacher at school to teach us fitness. But children watch and look up to their parents as they grow up. What we do at home as parents affect our children for a lifetime. So, if we do not exercise, then our children will not exercise.

Have you ever seen a man who look like he is 9 months pregnant? I have. I saw him in the mirror while looking at myself some years ago. It is not meant for a man to look like he is pregnant, nor is it healthy to be like that. So, what is going on in the body of a pregnant look - a- like man? Have you heard of Visceral Fat? It is body fat that is stored within the abdominal cavity and is therefore stored around many important internal organs such as the liver, pancreas and intestines. Storing excessive amounts of visceral fat is associated with increased risks of a number of health problems including type 2 diabetes.

Well what must one do to get rid of the pregnant look? You must make sure to do regular daily exercise. Yes, I said exercise, even if it's just walking - you should aim for 10,000 steps every day. I did it five days a week and I do not regret it. There is no way around it without exercising. I know you do not like the way you look, and I know you do not like the way you feel. Take it from me, I been there and know all the feelings that is associated with that pregnant look.

You should also have a healthy, balanced diet, eating largely plant-based foods. This will minimize your intake of animal fats and excess calories, but also ensure you get enough vitamins and minerals. Getting rid of that look requires 80 percent of eating healthy and 20 percent of exercising. What you put in your mouth really matters. So, remember that for you to get rid of that pregnant look, you must eat healthy and exercise, because I know you do not want heart disease, type

2 diabetes, insulin resistance and some cancers.

Good nutrition is a great place to start, but without exercise as a catalyst to make it work, you're just wasting your time. You see, without any exercise, good eating habits may have little or no bearing on your level of fitness. There are great benefits to exercise. It increases muscles, BMR or basal metabolic rate, reduces fat, increases your energy level, increases overall fitness and stamina, reduces the appetite and blood pressure.

There are many types of exercise programs that you can do. But make sure that you choose one that will deal with the cardiovascular (the heart and circulatory) system, strengthening (the muscular system) and flexibility (mobility of the joints). As you know the heart pumps blood throughout your body. And because the heart is a muscle, it can be strengthened as any other muscle in the body with exercise.

The body's muscular system is the primary factor in determining our "physique." And when we do not exercise these muscles, we tend to feel tight, with no energy and strength. Your muscles are very important to your body. For example: without back muscles, the spine would collapse under the weight of the head and shoulders. So, muscle strength is a critical factor in your overall health. So, while you are thinking about a good nutritional meal, do not forget a good exercise program which will make you feel and look better.

 REST

What do you think about when you hear the word rest or sleep? Many people think about weekends, lunch hour, vacations, going on a cruise, holidays, and sad to say church. Because many people come to church and go to sleep. Well any way I do not want to get into that. We must realize that rest is very important. Not only during weekends, etc. But every day we must get the proper amount of rest.

I have seen people literally deprive themselves of sleep. They would work all day and go to church five times a week. And then visit everybody in the hospital, while at the same time they do not eat right, exercise, or get proper rest. You cannot keep doing that and not get sick. If you are not resting properly you are abusing your body. When God created man, He added rest to his nature. Even Jesus had to stop and get some rest.

Sleeping is very important. During sleep, breathing is slower, deeper and more regular. Blood pressure and reflex irritability decrease, and most voluntary muscles relax. Sleep is very essential to life. So just like eating healthy and exercising is good for you, the proper amount of rest is good too.

Every night the average adult needs about 8 hours of sleep. And adults 65 years and older, need about 7 hours of sleep. Do not neglect your sleep time because it is very unhealthy. Rest can beat stress and help heal your body. So, rest every day no matter how busy you may be.

God has a way for us to stay healthy. If we eat, exercise, and rest properly, then we are doing what He wants us to do. Just remember, we are already healed, and we must maintain our healing.

# CHAPTER 4

## *Where Did It Come From*

In America alone, many people are suffering with all kind of diseases. It is sad to say that Christians are included in the masses of the sick and afflicted, when we are supposed to be examples of the healed. But in many cases the world is a better example than the body of Christ. Now in this chapter you are going to find out how different diseases started, and what types of foods contribute to these diseases.

Due to our reliance on convenience foods, Americans eat too much fat and too little fruit, vegetables and whole grains. As a result, we are now plagued by many degenerative diseases not found in those countries where the consumption of fruits and vegetables are much higher. Over 80 percent of the world's population today, does not consume the daily recommended amounts of 3 servings of fruit and 5 servings of vegetables. Did you know that 50 percent of all diseases are related to our diet, with 75 percent of all doctor visits linked to poor dietary habits? And over 80 percent of all black Americans will die and go to heaven from diseases related to poor eating habits.

There are many diseases that are obvious in the black community, including diabetes. Millions of Americans have acquired this disease that affects the eyesight, toes, feet, legs and extremities of the limbs. The odds of African Americans having diabetes is greater than white Americans, and this includes a high percentage of Christians.

There are two main types of diabetes: Type I (insulin dependent) diabetes, and Type II (non-insulin dependent) diabetes. Type I and Type II diabetes are quite different diseases. The goal of treatment for both are to keep the blood sugar level as close to normal as possible. Your blood sugar level is changing all the time. For people who do not have diabetes, the blood sugar level is between 70 - 140 mgldl, but this range varies from person to person.

Sugars and starches (carbohydrates) in food are changed by our bodies into a form of sugar called glucose, which enters the blood. This glucose or blood sugar, is the fuel for the body's work. A hormone called insulin is made by the pancreas. Insulin helps the sugar to enter each body cell, where it is used as needed for energy, or stored for later use. When the right amount of insulin is present at the right time, the right amount of sugar is used by the body.

In diabetes, the body is less able to change food into the energy your body needs. When you have diabetes, your body is not able to make enough insulin, or the insulin is not able to perform the process it should. The sugar cannot get into the body cells, so it builds up in the blood. Over time too much sugar in the blood can cause many problems.

Type I (insulin-dependent) diabetes occurs most often in children and teens, but it can begin at any age. In this type of diabetes, the cells in the pancreas that makes insulin, stops working. Thus, the body is not able to make insulin, stops working. Thus, the body is not able to make insulin. Without insulin, the sugar from food cannot be used for fuel. Sugar builds up to high levels in the blood.

Insulin injections are needed to treat type I diabetes. A treatment program which balances insulin, your own meal plan, and physical activity is prescribed.

The goal of treatment is to keep blood sugar within your target range. In order to do this, people who have type I diabetes must take insulin shots. Many people take insulin two or more time per day.

Type II (non-insulin dependent) diabetes occurs most often in people who are overweight and over the age of forty, although it can happen at any age or weight. Type II diabetes is much more common than type I diabetes. Over 90 percent of all people with diabetes, have Type II diabetes.

Most people with type II diabetes are overweight. Obesity is part of the initial cause of diabetes. The goal of treatment for people with type II diabetes is the same as that for those with type I diabetes. And that is to keep blood sugar levels in their target range while enjoying each day as much as possible. So, let us keep an eye on our weight and set a goal of getting it under control.

Whether you believe this or not, diabetes is the third leading cause of death in the United States. However, some people are still ignoring this fact and still eating foods that is raising their blood sugar levels. So please be careful of what you eat, especially in simple carbohydrates.

 ## HIGH BLOOD PRESSURE

### (Hypertension)

This disease has become a common occurrence among African Americans. An estimated 30 million Americans have high blood pressure, and African Americans have the highest percentage of all.

Just one 150 years ago, most African Americans had no choice but to eat the way they did. Many of them were very poor and could not afford certain foods. So, they ate what they had or the leftovers that were given to them. Most of us are still eating the way our slave parents ate. They did not have a choice, but we do. Slavery is over now, and it is time to break an old and deadly tradition. We have better jobs now. We are doctors, lawyers, nurses, governors, mayors, teachers, business owners etc. We do not have to eat like slaves any more.

Hypertension has taken hundreds of precious lives

each year. In urbanized societies, this disease is quite common among African Americans. High blood pressure (hypertension) will destroy the arterioles (the small terminal twigs of an artery that end in capillaries) in such organs as the liver, kidney, or brain and can also weaken the over worked heart. Many people suffer from heart failure, kidney failure, and strokes because of hypertension. Why is that? Because many families know they have a history of hypertension, but still will not take care of their bodies or change their diets. Also, obesity, high salt intake, smoking, and emotional and physical stress plays a big part in the susceptibility and effects of hypertension.

It is going to take a great deal of discipline on our part in order for us to overcome this deadly disease. It is treated with a self-help regimen that includes a no-salt diet and a weight-reducing diet, no smoking, an exercise program and the avoidance of, or more successful coping with stressful situations. I believe that if the saint of God would give up salt, and salty foods, lose weight, exercise, kick the smoking habit, and eat fresh fruit, vegetables and lean meat. By eating like this it is so possible that this disease can be history.

## ARTHRITIS

What comes to your mind when you hear the word arthritis? I think about old people, and people in the nursing home. Well, here is a disease that doesn't care about your age, color, creed or religion.

Arthritis is the inflammation of the joints and its effects thereof. In its acute form arthritis is marked by pain, inflammation, redness, and swelling. There are three principal forms of arthritis; Osteoarthritis, Rheumatoid arthritis, and Septic arthritis.

Osteoarthritis, also called osteoarthrosis, is a degenerative disease of the joints and an apparent consequence of the aging process. It is also thought to be a stress related disease associated with weight bearing afflicting over 15 million Americans.

Rheumatoid arthritis, is a chronic, progressive disease in which inflammatory changes occur throughout the connective tissues of the body. Most characteristically the process attacks the joints of the hands, feet, wrists, knees, hips, or shoulders. Rheumatoid arthritis is three times as common in women as in men and afflicts between one and three percent of the population in developed nations. Rheumatoid arthritis is often associated with physical or emotional stress; however, poor nutrition or bacterial infection may also be the cause. Its onset is most common between the ages of 25 and 50, but it also has been known to appear during childhood and among the elderly. It afflicts 2 million Americans.

Septic arthritis, is an acute inflammation of one or more joints, caused by infection.

 ## HEART DISEASE

This disease is always heart breaking when I talk about it. Because it brought tears to my eyes, while studying about it, I know that it is past the time for us to get the message out about this disease.

Your heart is the most important muscle in your body. Blood is pumped by the heart and circulated throughout the body through blood vessels. A normal heart is about the size of your first. It beats about 70 times a minute, or more than two one half billion beats in a life span of three score years and ten (70 years). An adult heart pumps about 6 ounces of blood at each stroke, or 5,000 gallons a day. The pulmonary artery carries blood to the lungs for oxygenation and the aorta carries blood to the rest of the body. This muscle is very unique and must be taken care of.

Heart disease is the leading health problem of the western world. It is the number one cause of death in the United States. Over 1 million lives taken annually by this terrible disease, and an estimated 60 million Americans are afflicted by heart disease. It saddens me to report that, African Americans lead the percentage of people affected by this disease also.

This is due to the fact that most African Americans eat too much fat, salt and sugar. With this type of life style everyday 1,440 people die from a heart attack. This is not a joke, nor is this something to be taken lightly. Even God knew that fat, salt and sugar was not good for us. In the bible God said do not eat fat (Deut. 7:22-23). Did you know that it's not even on God's menu?

There are many other diseases I did not mention that afflict babies, children and adults. But the few that I have mentioned are all too common. They are dangerous and even deadly, and I hope you take note of them.

# CHAPTER 5

## *How to Stay Healthy*

There are literally hundreds of published and recommended diet plans out now. But none of them work. I am sorry to say it this way, but I must be blunt. We have been fooled by the commercials on television and radio, newspapers and advertisement on billboards. People want to lose weight so bad, that they will try almost anything.

Diets will not keep you healthy. Missing meals and drinking a diet drink is not healthy. You do not cut back on putting gas in your car just because the price of gas has gone up. Gas is fuel for the car to run on. Likewise, food is fuel for the body. Therefore, you do not cut back on the fuel for the body to run on.

We have been taught to count and watch the calories we eat. And because of this, we take calculators to the grocery store. It has become another math course for us. And many of us just give up because it's so complicated. But I believe we are counting the wrong thing. We have been misled. And it is time for the truth to be heard. We need to be reeducated about losing weight, how to keep the weight off and the food we eat.

 REEDUCATE

Did you know that 75 percent of all Americans are overweight? Did you know that most of us are eating our way to heaven? Yes, it is a fact that we are fat, out of shape and unhealthy. In 2015 the American diet was comprised of 112.3 percent of red meat, and 62.7 percent of fat. It gets worse as we go on. Caloric sweeteners, total 137.5 percent, refined sugar 64.2 percent (white sugar, brown sugar, raw sugar, corn syrups, fructose, dextrose, all sugar substitutes, honey), coffee 26.7 percent, soft drinks 42.5 percent and pork 46. 3 percent and pork 46.3 percent. I hope you are taken this seriously.

Because you my friend, could be in those numbers.

No wonder heart disease is the number one cause of all death, and cancer is number two. Diseases of the heart were the leading cause of death with 35.7 percent of all deaths due to heart disease. Another 23.2 percent of the deaths were due to cancer. You heard the old saying "you are what you eat." But I have gotten a new one. "If you abuse it (your health), you lose it." Do not be a part of the statistics that I gave earlier. But be a part of those who are walking in good health.

 ## LOSING WEIGHT

I have talked and counseled with many people that are overweight. They all say that it is hard to lose weight and keep it off. But I always tell them it is not hard when you do it the right way. And the right way is to know what to eat and what not to eat. In other words, be conscious about what you eat. Do not just grab anything and eat it. Read labels to find out what is in the food you consume. Many of you have pets at home, and when you go to the store to purchase food for them you read the label to see what is in the food. However, when you purchase food for yourself or family, you grab the food and put it in the shopping cart. What a shame! We treat the cat, dog and even our automobile better than we do ourselves.

As I said earlier that we are counting the wrong thing. We are concentrating on one thing, when we should be looking at something else. I have said it once and I will say it again, Americans eat too much fat and too little fruit, vegetables and whole grains. It is not the calories that causes heart disease, and certain cancers. It is the fat that we eat. If we were more aware of the fat we eat, we would be much healthier and thinner.

Now let me help you understand how this fat thing work in our food. One gram of carbohydrates contains 4 calories. A gram of protein contains 4 calories. And a gram of fat contains 9 calories. For example, let's say you are eating a piece of cheese. The first thing you do is look at the fat content per serving. For example, one piece of cheese has 9 grams of fat, 110 calories and 440 milligrams of sodium. This is what you do, multiply the calories per gram that is in the fat by the total fat content in the cheese per serving. To make it simple, multiply the total fat by 9 (the number of calories in 1 gram of fat) and divide the answer by the total number of calories per serving and you will come up with the total number of the fat that is in the calories per serving.

Many of us have been counting the calories, but we never look out for the fat that we eat nor the calories that is in the fat. That one piece of cheese has enough fat in it that you would not need any more fat for the rest of the day. Let us look at one more food item. Two tablespoons of peanut butter have 190 calories, 6 grams of carbohydrates, 9 grams of protein, and 17 grams of fat. Now when you add up all the calories that are in the carbohydrates, protein and fat, it is enough to make anybody fat and sick sooner or later.

Fat is the most concentrated source of food energy and very necessary to health. Fat deposits provide insulation and protection for the body structure, as well as a storehouse for energy. Food fats are carriers of fat-soluble vitamins and include certain essential unsaturated fatty acids.

Saturated fats contain only single bond carbon linkages and are the least active chemically. They are usually solid at room temperature. Most animal fats are saturated. The common saturated fats are: acetic, butyric, caproic, capric, lauric, myristic, palmitic, stearic, arachidic, and behenic-butter fat, coconut oil, palm oil and peanut oil are high in saturated fats.

Unsaturated fats contain one or more double-bond carbon linkages and are usually liquid at room temperature. Vegetable oils and fish oils most frequently contain unsaturated fats. Hydrogenated oil is partially converted from naturally polyunsaturated fats to saturated fats and makes liquid oils partially solid. May adversely affect the levels of fat in the blood and has been linked to colon cancer in some reports (a consumer's dictionary of food additives).

We use margarine because we think it is better than butter. But did you know that hydrogenated oil is in it? And most of us who are trying to lose weight or stay healthy, overdo it with margarine anyway. I do not use butter or margarine at all. I have no use for it. It has fat, salt, and cholesterol in it and really bad for my blood and heart.

I am going to make a statement that may shock you . . . and I make any apologies for saying this. No one and I mean no one who is over weight is truly healthy. You will be more prone to exhaustion and shortness of breath and subject to have aches and pain in your joints and headaches. Being overweight causes you to have different illnesses: arthritis, diabetes, inflammation of the gall bladder, high blood pressure, heart disease, cirrhosis of the liver, hernias of various sorts, varicose veins, kidney disease and not to mention sexual problems. I am not trying to scare anyone. But it is time to eat healthy, lose the weight and keep it off.

I am going to share with you my secret on how you can lose weight and keep it off. You do not need a food scale nor a calculator anymore. This is not a diet plan, it is a life style. The first thing you do every night and every morning, is pray and ask God to help you though this. He is the one that will give you the ability, strength, and wisdom to achieve your goals. This is not in your own strength for it is God who is all the while effectually at work in you - energizing and creating in you the power and desire - both to will and do work for His good pleasure and satisfaction and delight (Phil. 2:13 amp.).

Second, know that you can lose weight and keep it off. You can do it. Just declare it: I can do all things through Christ which strengthened me (Phil. 4:13).

Third, everyday eat fresh fruit and vegetables (not canned). if you are going to eat meat, eat chicken, turkey, and fish (do not fry, and do not buy or eat packed lunch meat). Bake or broil the chicken without the skin. If you are going to eat cold cereal, buy it without sugar. When using milk, buy fat free milk, and stay away for a while from consuming cakes, ice cream, candy and pies, because it will harm you. If you want a good sugar substitute, use fruit and pure maple syrup. Maple syrup is low in calories, and it has calcium and a little iron in it. Do not forget to drink your water. We have been taught to drink 8 glasses of water every day. But the truth is adults should consume one ounce of water foe every two pounds of body weight daily.

    Fourth, get into a good exercise program. Everybody need to exercise, whether you are wonderfully old or tender young. It doesn't take much time to do this, just three times a week, 30 minutes per workout. You can do it!

    Fifth, every night when you lay down to sleep do not fall right to sleep. While you are laying there thinking about the Lord, visualize the body size you want it to be. See yourself fit and healthy. Meditate on it and then rest and sleep on it. By doing all of this you will cut your fat, salt, and sugar intake in a big way. But you must commit yourself to this in order for it to work. Remember this is not a diet plan. It is a life style.

## HOW TO KEEP THE WEIGHT OFF

As I said earlier, commit yourself to the plan that I have given you. But I must add a few more things to what I previously stated. You must avoid, stay away from and not buy certain foods that are not good for you. When various occasions occur (holidays, special events, etc.), do not change from your commitment that you had with yourself. Try to get someone else involved. Teach your family, friends and neighbors what you have learned. Do not worry about getting on a scale every day. Your clothes will reflect the weight loss.

 ## THE FOOD WE EAT

The next time you eat ask yourself these questions. Is this food truly ministering to my body? Will these fried foods make you stronger and better? Do I really think that soft drinks, and alcohol beverages are good for me? I know you do not believe that these foods I mentioned are good for you. So, since you do not believe it, stop eating foods that do not strengthen and build you up.

Our bodies need the nutrients to live a healthy life on this God given earth. From vitamin A to Z we must consume it every day to carry out our daily duties. Our eyes, skin, hair, and blood need us to eat food that have vitamin A to Z in it. I want to give you a break down on what these vitamins will do for you.

 ## VITAMIN A

Vitamin A is essential for night vision, and it promotes healthy skin and mucous, the production of red and white corpuscles in the blood, and for lactation, vitamin A is fat-soluble and is sensitive to oxygen, especially with heat. Collard greens, carrots, turnip greens, spearmint, parsley, spinach, sweet potatoes, kale, mustard greens, broccoli, papaya, and cantaloupe are rich in vitamin A.

 ## VITAMIN B1 (Thiamine)

Vitamin B1 is a vital element in the body's production of energy through the breakdown of carbohydrates and it is responsible for other metabolic reactions. It also appears to be necessary for the normal function of the nervous system and is involved in the action of the heart. Vitamin B1 is water-soluble and is sensitive to heat. Brewer's yeast, sunflower seeds, english walnuts, lima beans, kale, turnip greens, collards, raisins, baked potatoes, broccoli, cauliflower, pineapple, sweet potatoes, mustard greens, oats, lamb's quarters, spinach, green beans, leaf lettuce and oranges have high contents of vitamin B1.

##  VITAMIN B2 (Riboflavin)

Riboflavin is essential for cell growth and for enzymatic reactions by which the body metabolizes proteins, fats, and carbohydrates. It also helps to maintain healthy skin, eyes, and mucous membranes. Vitamin B2 is water-soluble and is sensitive to light, but not heat. Brewer's yeast, almonds (dried), wheat germ, sunflower seeds, lamb's quarters, turnip greens, broccoli, collards, kale, mustard greens, spinach, english walnuts, black walnuts, peas, lima beans, green beans, raspberries, barley are rich in vitamin B2.

## VITAMIN B6 (Pyridoxine)

Vitamin B6 takes part in many enzyme reactions and is particularly important to brain and nervous system functions. Vitamin B6 is water-soluble and is sensitive to oxygen and ultra violet light. Wheat bran, wheat germ, soy beans, indian corn, barley, rice (brown), cabbage, carrots are sources of vitamin B6.

 ## VITAMIN B12 (Cyanocobalamin)

There is little or no vitamin B12 found in plants. Vitamin B12 is necessary for proper functioning of body cells, particularly in the nervous system, the bone marrow and the gastrointestinal tract. It is also involved in the metabolism of fats, proteins and carbohydrates. Vitamin B12 is water-soluble and is sensitive to light, acids and alkalis.

Vitamin B12 is naturally found in animal products, including fish, meat, poultry, eggs, milk, and milk products. Vitamin B12 include clams, liver, fish, crab, low-fat beef and fortified cereal. Vitamin B12 is the largest and most complex vitamin currently known to man. A slight deficiency of vitamin

B12 can lead to anemia, fatigue, mania, and depression, while a long-term deficiency can cause permanent damage to the brain and central nervous system.

 ## VITAMIN C (Ascorbic Acid)

Vitamin C is a plant vitamin, occurring to some degree in almost all plants. The body neither makes nor stores vitamin C. A continuous supply must be provided in the food we eat. Normal body cell functioning requires ascorbic acid, as does the formation of healthy collagen (the basic protein of connective tissue), bones, teeth, cartilage, skin, and capillary walls. Vitamin C also promotes the body's effective use of other nutrients, such as iron, 13 vitamins, vitamins A and E, calcium, and certain amino acids. By promoting the formation of strong connective tissue, it helps to heal wounds and burns. Ascorbic acid is water-soluble and is sensitive to air, heat, light and copper ware.

Acerola (fruit), rosehips, wild strawberry (leaves), parley, green pepper, broccoli, spearmint, turnip greens, papaya, kale, collards, mustard greens, oranges, strawberries, lemons, garlic, cantaloupe, carrots, onions and spinach are excellent sources of vitamin C.

 ## VITAMIN D

Vitamin D does not occur in plants, but some plants do contain compounds called sterols, which can be irradiated with ultra violet light to make vitamin D. The human skin contains another sterol, which is converted to vitamin D by the ultra violet part of sun light. Other natural sources of vitamin D are: fish liver oils, milk, and egg yolk. Vitamin D is necessary for healthy bones and teeth, for proper assimilation and body balances of calcium and phosphorus, and for preventing rickets. It is fat-soluble and is not sensitive to heat, light, or oxygen.

 ## VITAMIN E

Vitamin E is an antioxidant, it acts in the body to protect red blood cells, vitamin A, and unsaturated fatty acids from oxidation damage. It also appears to help maintain healthy membrane tissue. Vitamin E is fat-soluble and is sensitive to oxygen, alkalis, and ultra violet light. Sunflower oil, cotton seed oil, wheat germ oil, walnuts, corn oil, olive oil, basil nuts, soybean oil, broccoli, spinach, asparagus, oatmeal, pecans, and apples are natural sources of vitamin E. Generally, it is found in whole grains and their oils, green leaves and seeds.

## VITAMIN K

Vitamin K occurs primarily in plants, it is synthesized by intestinal bacteria in the small intestine. Vitamin K is necessary for the synthesis by the liver of the blood clotting enzyme, prothrombin. It is fat-soluble and sensitive to light, oxygen, strong acids, and alcoholic alkalis. Sources of Vitamin k are: alfalfa, green leafy vegetables, soybean oil, cauliflower and tomatoes.

## NIACIN (Nicotinic Acid)

Niacin, a vitamin of the B complex occurs in both plant and animal tissue, but in different forms. The body changes the niacin from plant foods to niacinamide for use; animal foods contain niacinamide ready-made. Niacin takes part in enzyme reactions involved in the production of body energy and in tissue respiration. Niacin is water-soluble and is not sensitive to heat, acids or alkalis. Brewer's yeast, sunflower seeds, sesame seeds, wheat germ, rice (brown), whole wheat, almonds, parsley, peas, dates, figs, cashews, brazil nuts, potatoes, green beans, broccoli, sweet potatoes and turnip greens are excellent sources of niacin.

 ## PROTEIN (Amino Acids)

Amino acids when combined with nitrogen forms thousands of different proteins, are not only the units from which proteins are formed but are also the end products of protein digestion.

There are twenty-two known amino acids. Eight of these are called essential amino acids. These essential amino acids cannot like the others, be manufactured by the human body and must be obtained from food or supplements. A ninth amino acid, histidine, is considered essential only for infants and children. The eight necessary amino acids are found in foods of animal origin such as meats, poultry, seafood, eggs, milk, and cheese. Also, amino acids are found in seeds, nuts, peas, grains and beans.

 ## MINERALS

Our supply of minerals comes almost exclusively through the food chain. Plants take them from the ground and incorporate them into organic compounds that we consume by eating either the plants or the animals that ate the plants.

 ## CALCIUM

Calcium is necessary for healthy bones and teeth, for clotting of the blood, for the functioning of nerve tissue and muscles (including the heart), for enzymatic processes, and for controlling the movement of fluids through cell walls. Calcium dissolves in acid but is not affected by heat or light. Sources of calcium are: turnip greens, almonds, mustard greens, parley, figs collards, broccoli, maple syrup, spinach, cabbage, cauliflower, celery, kidney beans, leeks, lentils, oranges, and okra.

## CHLORINE

Chlorine is a poisonous gas, but in the form of chloride compounds, it is an essential mineral nutrient. Chloride acts with sodium to maintain the balance between fluids inside and outside cells. Gastric juice contains hydrochloric acid, the production of which requires chloride. Table salt (sodium chloride) is our main source, but is generally used to excess, with harmful results. Parsley, celery, bananas, coconut (fresh), kale, leaf cabbage, barley, turnip greens, sweet potatoes, leaf lettuce, hazelnuts, spinach, beets, carrot, and whole wheat contains chlorine.

 ## MAGNESIUM

Magnesium occurs in both plant and animal tissue. It is essential as an enzyme activator and is probably involved in the formation and maintenance of body protein. Cashews, soy beans, almonds, brazil nuts, lima beans, barley, peanuts, kidney beans, whole rye, pecans, whole wheat, oats, english walnuts, brown rice, collards, spinach, apples, asparagus, bananas, blackberries, cabbage, cucumbers, grapes, lemons, lettuce and tomatoes contain magnesium.

 ## PHOSPHORUS

Phosphorus takes part in the production of energy for the body, and it is second only to calcium as a constituent of bones and teeth. Phosphorus is necessary for metabolic functions relating to the brain and nerves, as well as for muscle action and enzyme formation. Wheat germ, sunflower seeds, sesame seeds, almonds, brown rice, kelp, whole wheat, soy beans, parley, cauliflower, broccoli, potatoes, sweet potatoes, kale, spinach, collards, asparagus, celery, apple, barley, garlic and tomatoes are sources of phosphorus.

 ## POTASSIUM

Potassium is abundant in both plant and animal tissue. It promotes certain enzyme reactions in the body, and it acts with sodium to maintain normal ph levels and balance between fluids inside and outside cells. Kelp (edible), blackstrap, molasses, parley, sunflower seeds, wheat germ, almonds, dates, bananas, soy beans, potatoes, mustard greens, collards, cantaloupe, cherries, eggplant and watermelon are good sources of potassium.

## SODIUM

Sodium regulates the volume of body fluids and balanced with potassium, maintains pressure equilibrium between fluids outside cells and those inside. Kelp, irish moss, dulse, celery, spinach, kale, turnips, mustard greens, carrots, and whole wheat are sources of sodium.

## SULFUR

Sulfur is involved in bone growth, blood clotting, and muscle metabolism. It also helps to counteract toxic substances in the body by combining with them to form harmless compounds. Foods containing sulfur include: soybeans, kidney beans, oats, lima beans, whole wheat, black walnuts, whole rye, onions, asparagus, garlic, sesame seeds, sunflower seeds.

COPPER

Copper occurs in both plant and animal tissue. It is essential with iron for the formation of hemoglobin in red blood cells; and it is important for protein and enzyme formation, as well as for the nervous and reproductive systems, bones, hair, and pigmentation. Currants, legumes, mushrooms, nuts, and raisins contain copper.

 IODINE

Iodine occurs dependable only in seafood and seaweeds. Iodine is necessary for normal physical and mental growth and development, as well as for lactation and reproduction. Iodine is found in pulse, Irish moss, and kelp.

 IRON

Iron is essential to form the oxygen carrying hemoglobin in red blood cells and it is also involved in muscle functioning and in enzyme reactions for producing energy. Sources of Iron include: Kelp, wheat germ sunflower seeds, parley, black walnuts, almonds, spinach, mustard greens, soybeans, maple syrup, broccoli, apples, blueberries, cabbage, grapes, oats, potatoes, whole wheat.

## MANGANESE

Plants are the best sources of manganese. Traces of this metal are necessary in the body for healthy bones and for enzyme reactions involved in the production of energy. Manganese is found in bran, whole grains, nuts, green leafy vegetables and wheat germ.

## ZINC

Zinc occurs in animal tissue, and in plants when grown in good soil. It is important for various enzymatic reactions, for the reproduction system, and the manufacture of body protein. Bran, nuts, green leafy vegetables are sources of zinc. (The Herb Book, John Lust and Vitamin Bible, Earl Mindell)

# CHAPTER 6

## *Let's Talk*

There are so many things I want to share with you. Which is why I decided to commit this chapter to you. Maybe this will help you understand why I am writing this book. After reading this I believe you will begin to see and feel the burden I have, and how much I really love and am concerned people.

I have a burden for you. One reason is because I am your brother and I know the struggles we go through. I know our culture, background, and traditions. And I am sick and tired of hearing that we are the number one victims of most diseases. Many of us still cannot see the light. Some of us do not want to change. But whether you want to or not, it is time for a change.

Most of us have a concern about what color Adam and Eve were. And most of us believe they were people of color instead of being a white man. And we are very proud that they were people of color, because it gives us a sense of identity. However, I have a concern, if we with pride say that Adam was black, why don't we eat like him and keep our bodies healthy, fit and strong? As a matter of fact, Adam was very healthy and productive, even in his old age. By the time most of us reach forty, we are suffering with different type of diseases. We are neither strong, active or productive. You see the older you get the stronger you are supposed to be. So, if you are so proud that the first man on earth was black, you need to be proud that he took good care of his body and left an excellent example of how we should eat and be strong, even at an old age.

Somehow, we as a people got off course. Black people in history used to eat foods that would build and strengthen their bodies. They would eat fresh fruit and vegetables, herbs, beans etc. They even knew what kind of roots and herbs would help them when they got sick. They lived much longer than we live now. Sicknesses such as diabetes, heart disease and high blood pressure was not even in the picture because we were just a healthy people. But somehow, we got off course.

History said our fore-fathers would educate their families about God, family hood, wealth, food and how to stay healthy. They would not allow their children to just eat anything, no matter how good it looked or tasted. They did not let other people, nations or tribes dictate what they should eat. A matter of fact, we used to teach other nations how to eat and stay healthy. We were a special people that took diligent care of ourselves.

Well, somehow, we got diluted and polluted in the western world and its culture. In the beginning, we used to teach other people. Now the television, advertising companies, and our society instruct us now. We do not care about ourselves anymore, and family values have gone down. We have forsaken God and His statutes and replaced it with western world values. We do not eat like kings and queens anymore, but eat like slaves, and our new slave master is the fast food restaurant and television. I am sorry if I sound like I am upset, but really, I am not. I believe it is time that somebody tell it like it is.

When we read the newspaper and watch reports on television about the number of blacks that are dying from different diseases, for some reason we still will not change. We hear that black women develop heart disease 2 1/2 times more often than white women. Black women have high blood pressure twice as often as white women. An estimated 40 percent of black women older than 40 have high blood pressure, a major risk factor for stokes. Nearly 50 percent of black women are considered obese, or at least 30 percent above their ideal weight. Black women die of cancer twice as often as white women. Breast cancer, cancer of the uterus and almost one third of the cancer deaths occurred in black women in 2017. Whites have a 53 percent chance of surviving cancer; blacks have a 38 percent chance. And black women are less likely to have adequate preventive medical care or screening for these cancers. Black women die from diabetes complications three to four times more often than white women. This mean my black sisters must change or else we (black brothers) will not have a mother, sister, and wife. For us to wipe out the diseases, we must break these unhealthy habits, bad traditions, and get back to the basics. We got to stop eating our way to heaven right now.

## BAD HABITS

Bad eating habits is the cause of most of our diseases, and as black people we have bad eating habits that result in sickness or death. Many of our black brothers and sisters have high blood pressure that is out of control, because they cannot stop eating salty foods. The sad thing about this is when the doctor tells us not to eat certain foods because of diabetes, heart disease, high blood pressure etc., we still go on eating the food the doctor tell us not to eat.

Unhealthy habits begin when we are infants. Many black mothers feed their babies the wrong food. The same foods and beverages that we are addicted to, we feed to our babies. By the time our babies are 2 and 3 years old, they have cavities because of the junk foods we allow them to eat. Most of our kids are overweight. They are always sick with colds and have all types of allergic reactions. We must break these unhealthy habits my black brothers and sisters. And we can do it . . . with the help of God.

##  BAD TRADITIONS

Every fourth of July we get out the old Bar-B-Que pit and slap some ribs on it. Pies, cakes, and ice cream is always there to conclude our great feast. Let us not forget the holiday that everybody loves Thanksgiving. Oh my, my, my, honey we just got to get us some chitterlings, hog maws, glazed ham, fried chicken, and do not forget those sweet potato pies, chocolate cake and make sure you buy some candy, nuts and fruit for the kids and for our company that is coming over. Now doesn't that menu look familiar? I didn't even list some of the other foods we eat on Thanksgiving, and there are many more believe me. And for most of us, we do not buy enormous quantities of fruit until Thanksgiving, and to tell you the truth about that it is to decorate our table instead of eating. What a shame. These are traditions that we've held onto for years. Now I am not against you celebrating different holidays but let us be real about this. What I am trying to say is the way we celebrate the holiday is the issue. When we begin to abuse our health and kill ourselves in the name of holidays, then that is when we need to change our traditions.

##  BACK TO THE BASICS

Good moral family values, education, taking care of your body and serving God is what we must do. Listen black brother and sister, getting back to the basics will destroy all these diseases, and we can even live longer to fulfill our purpose as a people. However, we must live a healthy, prosperous and longer life to bring it to pass.

Take care of yourself black man and open your eyes and see. Unstop your ears so you can hear. Prepare your heart to be used by God. Just get ready for the breaking of the day. I truly love you black man and I want you to make it with God's help. I truly love everybody with all my heart, no matter what your skin tone is. In God's eyes we are one race, human race. However, there is a reality about the dark skin people in America. We are eating our way to heaven by not taking care of business with our lives.

*"By eating many fruits and vegetables in place of fast food and junk food, people could avoid obesity. It is never too late to change the way you eat – once you do, your body will thank you with a longer and healthier life. (David H. Murdock)*

Getting back to the basics is key in not eating your way to heaven. Everybody wants to live a long happy healthy life and all the goods that come with it. Well stop what you're doing and ask yourself am I making it too complicated or am I keeping it basic with my spiritual, mental, and physical health? Only you know the answer to the question, however my prayer is that you made the chose to keep it basic.

Life is too short in abusing the greatest gift one could have, your health.

# CHAPTER 7

## *Good Recipes*

Here are a few recipes that are wholesome and good for you. Try them, I am sure you'll like them.

## Stir-Fry Vegetables with Brown Rice

### Ingredients

| | | |
|---|---|---|
| 1 | - | Pound fresh broccoli |
| 2 | - | Tbsp. walnut or corn oil |
| 1 | - | Onion, chunked |
| 1/3 | - | Cup soy sauce |
| 2 | - | Red bell peppers, chunked |
| 1/2 | - | Pound fresh mushrooms, quartered |
| 2 | - | Cups of cold brown rice |
| 2 | - | Tbsp. water |

Cut broccoli florets into bite-size pieces and peel stalks into thin slices. Heat oil in hot wok or large skillet over high heat. Add broccoli and onion, stir fry 1 minute. Add bell peppers and mushrooms. Stir-fry 2 minutes. Add soy sauce. Cook, stirring until vegetables are coated with sauce. Serve the vegetables over brown rice.

### Cabbage 'n Corn Soup

Servings: 4 to 6     Time:  30 minutes

**Ingredients**

| | | |
|---|---|---|
| 1 | - | Tsp. oil |
| 1 | - | Onion, sliced |
| 1 | - | Small cabbage, thinly sliced (about 6 cups) |
| 2 | - | Carrots, diced |
| 3 | - | Ears corn, cut off the cob |
| 2 | - | Pieces wakame (cabbage) or ¼ cup dulse (optional) |
| 6 | - | Cups water |
| 2/3 | - | Tbsp. miso or sea salt, to taste |

Heat oil in soup pot. Sauté onion, cabbage and carrots until soft and sweet-smelling, about 10 minutes. Add corn cut off the cob, water and wakame or dulse. (Soak wakame 10 minutes and cut into small pieces). Simmer 15 to 20 minutes until the vegetables are tender but haven't lost color. Season with miso or sea salt.

## Red Lentil-Squash Soup

Servings: 6 or more    Time:   45 to 60 minutes

**Ingredients**

| | | |
|---|---|---|
| 1 | - | tsp. sesame oil |
| 1 | - | onion, diced |
| 1/2 | - | squash, cubed (2 to 3 cups) |
| 1 | - | cup red lentils, cleaned and washed |
| 6 | - | cups water or strip kombu |

Heat oil; sauté onion and squash 2 to 3 minutes; add pinch of cumin. Pick through red lentils carefully. Rinse in strainer. Add to squash and onions. Pour in water and add bay leaves; bring to boil and simmer 45 minutes until soft and creamy. Remove bay leaves. Season with sea salt or miso.

## Baked Fish with Mushroom Sauce

Servings: 4 to 6     Time:    20 minutes

**Ingredients**

| | | |
|---|---|---|
| 1 | - | large fish fillet (1 ½ to 2 pounds) haddock, scrod, or halibut |

**Marinade:**

| | | |
|---|---|---|
| 1 | - | Tbsp. mustard (optional) |
| 1 | - | Tbsp. mirin or sake' |
| 1 | - | Tsp. shoyu or pinch of sea salt |
| 1 | - | Tbsp. lemon juice |
| 1/2 | - | Tsp. dill, oregano or basil leaves |
| 1 | - | Tsp. oil |

Rinse fish; place in oiled baking dish. Mix marinade; spread over fish. Allow to marinate in refrigerator until guests arrive, no longer than 1 hour. Cover and bake at 350 degrees F. for 15 to 20 minutes, depending on thickness of fish. When fish flakes easily, it is ready. Do not overcook. Pour sauce over fish and garnish; serve immediately.

## Mushroom Sauce

### Ingredients

| | | |
|---|---|---|
| 8-12 | - | Ounces fresh mushrooms, sliced |
| 1 | - | Tsp. oil |
| 1-2 | - | tbsp. kuzu dissolved in water |
| 2 | - | cups water or stock |
| | - | Pinch of sea salt to taste or 2 tsp. shoyu |

Slice mushrooms. Heat oil in fry pan; add mushrooms and stir. The heat should be hot enough to scar or brown the mushrooms to keep them from losing water and to enhance their flavor. Continue to sauté on high heat for 2 to 3 minutes, stirring often so they do not burn. Lower flame when mushrooms are tender. Dissolve kuzu in water, add to mushrooms; stir until thick and clear. Season with shoyu or sea salt.

# CHAPTER 8

## *Testimonies*

I love the passion that Bishop RJ Shackleford has for people of all colors. His teaching on health has changed my life. I have been suffering with being obese for most of my life. But listening to his teaching on how to live a healthy life has put me in a new mind set. I have lost 75 pounds and feel so good about myself.

-Sandra P. NY

Seven years ago, my mother was diagnosed with having sugar diabetes. Her sugar was so out of control that she was going back and forth to the hospital. Mother did not have the motivation in doing the right thing in getting healthy. But two years ago, I had mother listen to a message by Bishop Shackleford. Her life was never the same after listening to that powerful message. Now mother's weight is down, and her sugar is in control. Thank you Bishop Shackleford!

-Brenda D. MI

I can't believe I lost 55 pounds in such a short time. I have been struggling with my weight for a long time. But the moment I got connected with the ministry of Bishop Shackleford, my life has not been the same.

-Tony M. OH

I love food with a passion, unfortunately I like eating food that will make me terribly sick. My life was like a rollercoaster with trying to eat and exercise every day. But after attending one of Bishop Shackleford's health seminars, my life was turned around for the better. Now I have the tools to live a healthy and balanced life. Thank you Bishop Shackleford for your passion and love for people.

-Timothy J. MI

# CHAPTER 9

## *Change Your Mind*

If I had a dollar for every time I hear someone say, "I'm going to start eating healthier, get my mind right and exercise tomorrow." I would be a very wealthy man. So many of us get excited when we see on the infomercials about the new exercise toy. We even go as far as picking up the telephone to order that new toy. The telephone gets a big workout when you call your friends and love ones to tell them that you ordered a new exercise toy to start your exercise program.

The question for today, what will it take for you to live the best life ever? Well, let me put it like this, it will take more than getting excited about a new exercise toy. It will take more than being motivated. It will take more than calling your friends and love ones to tell them you are going to start living the good life tomorrow. I was raised around people who would always say "tomorrow is not promised to you." I am a firm believer that tomorrow is not promised to you. I know for sure that words of excitement that comes from your mouth will not change nothing unless we change our mind.

When I was a little boy my best friend in school had a nick name "bread." Everybody at school would see him on the playground during recess, playing and eating bread at the same time. When it was time to break for lunch, Bread would go around and ask the kids for their bread. Most of the kids would give their bread away to my best friend, and he would gladly take the bread and eat some right during lunch and save some for the recess. Now you know why we called my best friend Bread.

What a shocking surprise I got after 35 years in seeing Bread. He showed up at one of my meetings I had in Dallas, Texas. I did not recognize Bread because of his physical appearance. The meeting was such an enormous success base on what Bread told me. First, he said the love for eating bread really changed my life for the worse. After so many years of consuming so much bread with everything I ate, the weight gain began to take over, and the bad part about this I became a diabetic. Second, he made promises after promises that he will change his life around, but with every attempt he failed.

Bread told me after the meeting was over that he will never be the same. I ask what happened during the meeting? He said your love and passion for the wellbeing of others were so contagious and compelling that it made me change my mind forever. He said I will never ever be sick again. My mind is completely made up to get healthy.

One year later after seeing Bread at the meeting, I received something in the mail that brought tears in my eyes. Bread had sent me an 8x10 photo of himself and his wife. He had written a message on the back of the picture stating that he had lost 210 pounds. He is no longer take insulin and now mentor other people who are dealing with some of the same problems he dealt with. The last words on the back of the picture was "with a changed mind you can do anything."

A changed mind can move mountains. Your mountain may be an illness in your physical body. It may be a mental situation that has stopped you from accomplishing remarkable things in your life. Your mountain may be that you procrastinate, and it has caused you to stall in life. Your mountain may be food. Whatever your mountain is, with a changed mind you can accomplished anything. I am reminded about a passage in the Bible: Now to him who is able to do immeasurably more than all we ask or imagine, according to his power that is at work within us. Ephesians 3:20

There must be a paradigm shift for us to stop doing things that is keeping millions of people from enjoying a prosperous life. We must be reprogramed in our mind to overcome poverty, sickness, fear, mental instability and unhealthy eating. Our mind needs a new software to do the new things that will make us better. We have been living on the old program system for too long and it is killing so many people year after year. My mother use to say, "enough is enough." It is time for the shift to take place.

What are paradigms? For the most part, paradigms are multiple habits that are resident in our subconscious mind. Most of our habits has been handed down to us through our childhood life. Paradigms are programs in our subconscious mind which controls 95% of our behavior. These programs tell you what to eat, wear, what show to watch on television on a daily routine, and even how to drive your car. Paradigms are invisible, but you can see them through your behavior. Our paradigm tells us to live a contain way because it was handed down to do so. Our paradigm tells us to talk a contain way because of our home environment. Paradigm is culture, and culture ain't nothing but group habit, and group habit is paradigm. Your paradigm will tell you what to do whether it is right or wrong. However, our conscious mind is where our intellect is resident, but the part that control our behavior and moves us into action is our subconscious mind.

So now we know why we do what we do at home, work, church, and around our friends. We can't help but to eat unhealthy and not exercise on a regular basis. It is almost impossible for you to live a well-balanced life when your mind is totally controlled by the old program. The old program said be a negative person: be a lazy person, be a time waste person, have a poverty mentality, and a greedy person. You can't fix the problem with the same mind that broke it. You must change your mind for things to change.

## HOW TO CHANGE YOUR MIND

As I write this book, I am thinking about the multitude of people who really want to change their mind, but do not know where to begin. I truly understand how it feels when you want to do better but keep failing over and over along the way. My heart goes out to those who really want to stop the madness in having a destructive life style. Every day you say to yourself that you will change from eating your way to heaven to living the life God intended for you to live. I got some good news for you. Your life is about to change for the better. It will start after you learn how to renew your mind.

 ## FEED YOUR MIND

Our bodies need clean wholesome food to stay strong and healthy. However, in our society it is a little hard for some of us because we have fast food restaurants everywhere. Also, in today's world we are too busy to prepare and cook healthy food. Every time we turn on the television we see the many commercials advertising good tasteful food from restaurants that is so unhealthy for us. So just like we need to feed our bodies clean wholesome food, we need to feed our mind clean wholesome mental food every day.

Yes, our mind must feed on healthy thoughts, good books, healthy mind moving audios, positive affirmations, and sound meditation. You heard people say if you put your mind to it then you can do anything you want. Well it is true. A mind that is healthy will allow you to achieve anything in this world. Our action and behaviors are the blossom of our thoughts. You are what you think about all the time. Your action is eating five slices of cake at 2:00 A.M. in the morning only because you have been thinking about that cake all evening. So, a person thinks, so is that person. Therefore, you must feed, feed, feed, one more time, feed your mind the best mental food to overcome those bad thoughts that is keeping you from being healthy spiritually, mentally, and financially.

At one point in my life I was very unhealthy, not because of the food I was eating per say. It was my unhealthy thoughts that made me sick, overweight, negative, and without money. I was feeding my mind so much bad mental food in such way that my life was like the worse roller coaster ride ever. *"By thought, the thing you want is brought to you. By action, you receive it, . . ."* (*Wallace Wattles*)

I had to stop the madness because I was eating my way to heaven on the fastest freeway of life. When I looked in the mirror, I saw a very sick and unhappy person who was uncertain about my present and future life. Therefore, I had to say to myself "the main thing is to keep the main thing . . . main thing.' And the main thing for me was my wellbeing.

I thought about what my favorite writer said;

*"The intensity of your desire will depend on the clearness with which you picture to yourself what you want to be."* (*Wallace Wattles*)

I had to get a clear picture of what I wanted in my thought. I wanted peace, happiness, health and plenty of money. It was time to find the most quality and potent mental food to live on. I begin to feed on the greatest book that was ever written, the Bible. The narratives live of common people, and the example of Jesus Christ in the Bible brought new life in my mind. Reading became my new love in life because of how it made me feel. My desire to change got stronger and stronger every time I picked up a book to read. I would read to educate myself on books about health, finance, leadership, food, marriage, and spirituality. By feeding my mind, I begin to experience a paradigm shift.

The way you learned how to ride a bicycle is the same way you change your paradigm. You got on your bike to learn how to ride when you were a younger person and you did this repetitiously until it became lodge in your subconscious mind. You will change your paradigm by doing the new thing over and over until it becomes second nature. Repeating positive affirmations several times a day is like feeding your mind, and by doing this daily exercise will change your paradigm. Remember that *"a paradigm is multiple habits that is lodge in your subconscious mind."* (*Bob Proctor*)

 STRENGTHEN YOUR BODY

*"Take care of your body, it's the only place you have to live."* (*Jim Rohn*) What if I bought you your dream car that you always wanted? Also, let's say that will be your last car in life. What will you do with that car? Let me answer the question for you . . . take good care of that car because you know it will be your last and only car. Well, you only get one body in a life time, so love it, feed it, and strengthen your body. You are the

only one who can map out a life plan for you to follow, it's your body. If you don't design your own life plan, chances are you'll fall into someone else's plan. And guess what they have planned for you? Not much. Going day after day without strengthening your spiritual body. Mental body, and your physical body is like living with your fingers cross. We are made for growth and when we stop growing then we are eating our way to heaven.

It really doesn't take much to start the process in strengthening your body. Let's say you want to use walking as your exercise workout but have not used this form of exercise in a while. You can start walking around in your home or outside for one block. The more you walk the stronger your body will become and before you know it, your body will tell you to take longer walks. Walking is the easiest exercise out of all the body disciplines out there. No matter how old you may be, get up and do the simplest exercise there is.

Believe it can be done, because when you believe, your mind will find a way to do it. *"Thoughts become things. If you see it in your mind, you will hold it in your hand."* (*Bob Proctor*) Just believe that you have a strong body and your mind will go to work for you. Every day I say out loud to myself "every day in every way I am getting better." I truly believe what I tell myself and believe it or not, my body get right in line with what I believe. When you have a strong mind and a strong spirit, you got to have a strong body. When you have a strong body, it means you are putting quality food in it and doing some regular body disciplines. So, know for sure that a strengthening body help change your paradigm.

 ## FIND A ROLE MODEL

A mentor or role model is someone who sees more talent and ability within you, than you see in yourself, and helps bring it out of you. Believe me or not, a role model will help you change your mind from thinking average. We were created to be better than average, mediocre, and nonproductive. When your mind is stuck in the mud of tradition a good role model will help you get out the mud. You have been trying to change the way you eat but failed every time. You have been trying to stop smoking cigarettes but failed every time. You have been trying to get your finances in order but failed every time. A role model is the answer in overcoming our failures. He or she can help pull the best out of us even if you can't see best in yourself.

I am where I am because of my good role models who has helped shaped my life. My dad was my first role model and yes, he left a great impact on my life. I remember when I was a little boy dressed in a suit and tie, I told my dad that I wanted to preach just like him. Also, I wanted to sing and play the guitar like him. I would sit and watch my dad whenever he does something like preach, fix something that is broke, or how he interact with people. He told me because you are my son, I will guild you to be a good strong man. My dad truly kept his word with me and I am so glad. I am now a preacher just like him and I play the guitar too. My dad would eat so healthy when I was much younger and now I am health conscious. There is life changing power in having a role model.

It doesn't make any sense to have a role model if you will not listen to him/her and follow their orders. Your old program in your mind will not change if you do not follow orders. One of my associates wanted to stop being so bitter against her husband and start treating him like a loving wife should. So she found her a good mentor/role model to get herself in order with her husband. The role model told her what she needed to do and start immediately. The wife started doing her homework, but it only last for five days. The sad thing about this, she tried to make her role model think that she was still following orders, but her role model new that she was lying to herself. We must follow through with our role model to succeed.

My next role model only had two months of high school education. His annual income was four thousand dollars with no background in business nor any formal education. However, I think he is one of the wisest role models and a man of integrity that I can think of. Most of you know my role model and have seen him on television helping so many people live the God kind of life. He is Mr. Bob Proctor. I am a much better man spiritually, mentally, physically, and financially after listening and following his instructions. My mind set has changed tremendously by studying Bob Proctor in such a way that I feel like a brand-new person. I can never eat my way to heaven with the role models that is in my life.

## REPETITION IS POWERFUL

Do you want to be in the best health ever? What about wanting your annual income to become your monthly income? Are bad habits controlling your life? Well, your life can change in your favor right now when you use the power of repetition. Doing something positive and new over and over will turn you into the new person that you wanted. You can lose unwanted weight. You can stop eating unhealthily and start eating like a real king and queen should eat. You can start your new business and put other people to work. You are unstoppable by using the power of repetition. To change the old program in your mind is to do the new right thing repeatedly.

Repetition is reprogramming your subconscious mind with new possibilities. If you want to change your behaviors and the results you are getting, you must program a new idea into your subconscious mind. *"Whatever we plant in our subconscious mind and nourish with repetition and emotion will one day become a reality."* (*Earl Nightingale*)

Think about an area in your life that you want to change. Create a strong and powerful statement and write it out, at least once a day for the next ninety days say it out loud.

Write your statement like this, see examples below;

I am so happy and grateful now that, every day in every way I am getting better and better. Make sure your statement is written in the present tense. The reason you must say this statement out loud for ninety days, is that it takes ninety days to confirm a new habit. You can also say, I am so happy and grateful now that, I have peace, happiness, good health, and plenty of money. If you follow my orders your life will never be the same. Bad habits and old mind set will leave you like a bad cold that you caught, and you know that the cold will leave your body in a few days. Do not consider other people thoughts about your new way of living. Some will not understand what you are doing because it looks and sound strange to them, just keep on moving forward and enjoy the ride.

## Selected Bibliography

- Lovett, C. S., Help Lord, The devil wants me fat: Personal Christianity. California, 1977
- Berry, Linda, Internal Cleansing, Botanica Press. California, 1985
- Balch, James, F., Balch, Phyllis, A., Nutritional Healing, Avery Publishing Group Inc. New York, 1990
- Winter, Ruth, Food Additives: Crown Publishers. New York, 1989
- Mindell, Earl, Vitamin Bible: Warner Books. New York, 1985
- Lust, John, the Herb Book Bantam Books. New York, 1974
- Dufty, William, Sugar Blues: Warner Books. New York, 1975

- Estella, Mary, Natural Foods: Japan Publications, Inc., Tokyo andNew York, 1985
- Bieler, Henry G., Food is Your Best Medicine: Random House, Inc.
- Jensen, Bernard, Love Sex and Nutrition: Avery Publishing Group Inc. New York, 1988
- Lance, Kathryn, Low-Impact Aerobics: Crown Publishers, Inc. New York 1988
- Royal Penny C., Herbily Yours: Sound Nutrition, Utah, 1982

# ABOUT THE AUTHOR

*Robert J. Shackleford*

 Robert J. Shackleford is the founder of Bishop R.J. Shackleford Ministries and have been pastoring for 30 years. He is now under the leadership and direction of his dad Bishop Robert L. Shackleford Sr. of Greater Whole Truth Church of Detroit, Michigan. He has a special commission and calling to the church and world to teach the gospel of the kingdom of God and to teach balance in our lives.

He began to do some in-depth study on what makes the body function and what make the body breakdown. He also studied and did research on diverse types of food for several years. But what really amazed him about the body, food, and health, is what God's word say. Robert J. Shackleford has studied the scriptures and found out that God wants us to be stewards of our body.

He has been a vegetarian for many years and has studied intently about how to take care of the body and the types of food and herbs that attribute to good health. The ministry of this anointed man of God is in great demand throughout the body of Christ.

www.ingramcontent.com/pod-product-compliance
Lightning Source LLC
LaVergne TN
LVHW051842080426
835512LV00018B/3029